PUTTING ON THE BRAKES

Young People's Guide
to Understanding
Attention Deficit
Hyperactivity Disorder
(ADHD)

PATRICIA O. QUINN, M.D.
AND
JUDITH M. STERN, M.A.

Illustrations by
MICHAEL CHESWORTH

MAGINATION PRESS • WASHINGTON, DC

To our families: Joe, Joseph, Timothy, Patrick, Tara and
Uzi, Talia, Naomi

Photographs by Sandy Kavalier and Edward Max, M.D.

Library of Congress Cataloging-in-Publication Data
Quinn, Patricia O.
   Putting on the brakes : young people's guide to understanding
attention deficit hyperactivity disorder (ADHD) / by Patricia O.
Quinn and Judith M. Stern.
      p.   cm.
   Summary: A guide to understanding and gaining control over
attention deficit hyperactivity disorder.
   ISBN 0-945354-32-0 (paper) 0-945354-73-8 (Spanish ed.)
   1. Attention deficit disorders—Treatment—Juvenile literature.
   2. Hyperactive child syndrome—Treatment—Juvenile literature.
   3. Cognitive therapy for children—Juvenile literature.
   [1. Attention deficit disorders.   2. Hyperactive child syndrome.]
   I. Stern, Judith M.   II. Title.
   RJ496.A86Q56   1991
   618.92'8589—dc20   91-20390
                                                                CIP
                                                                 AC

Published by Magination Press, an imprint of the Educational Publishing
Foundation, American Psychological Association, 750 First Street, NE,
Washington, DC 20002; 1-800-374-2721.

Manufactured in the United States of America

10

CONTENTS

◆

FOREWORD FOR PARENTS
AND PROFESSIONALS

♦

When young people learn they have attention deficit hyperactivity disorder (ADHD), they have many questions, doubts, and fears. This book, written from both a pediatric and an educational perspective, attempts to address their needs and questions. School-age children respect material they find in a book, especially when it confirms or elaborates what they have learned from experience or from a significant adult. Children need reassurance that the problems they have are not unique to them. They benefit from a sense that help is available and that they themselves can be a powerful force in their own treatment.

This book attempts to give ADHD kids a sense of control and a perception of obtainable goals. It is not meant to replace professional guidance and consultation, which should be an ongoing process in the life of the ADHD child. It is important to keep the hopeful message of this book in mind in reading and talking together with ADHD kids.

The book was designed to be used with young people between the ages of 8 and 13. By reading the book together with their ADHD child, parents can open an ongoing discussion that will provide information and reassurance. Depending on reading ability, the book may be read by the child alone or out loud by an adult. Efforts have been made to explain unfamiliar or difficult words. A glossary has been provided so that the reader may conveniently look up any unfamiliar words as often as necessary.

It is recommended that the book be read and discussed in sections, in order to avoid overwhelming the ADHD child with too much information all at once. By providing frequent opportunities to discuss the content of the pages, an adult can help the child manage what is being covered. These discussions can be used to clear up misunderstandings, share personal insights, or raise further questions.

ADHD kids should be encouraged to read the book a number of times, as they may absorb additional meaning each time. The book can also be shared with siblings and friends, with the guidance of an informed adult. A parent, teacher, or counselor could be an effective partner in helping the child work through this book. In addition, with the help of a professional, this book could be effectively used by a small group of children who are engaged in the process of learning about their attention deficit hyperactivity disorders.

PART I
♦
UNDERSTANDING ADHD

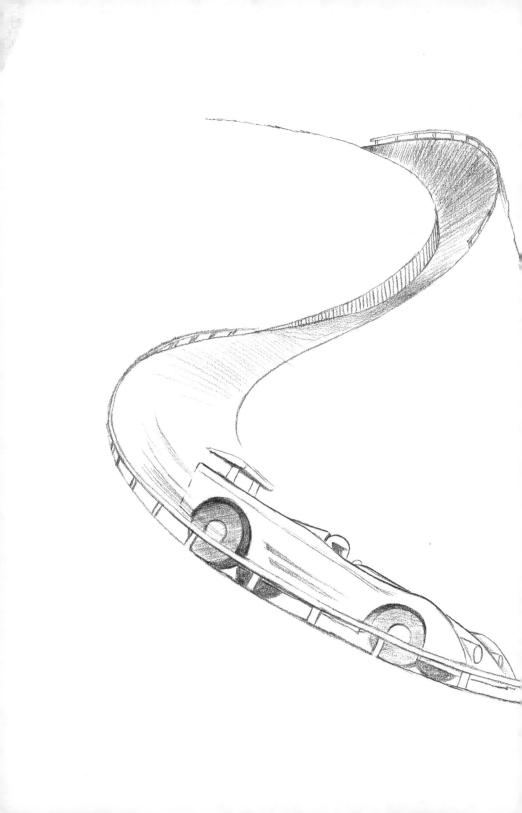

1.

WHAT IS ADHD ALL ABOUT?

Imagine a slick, hot, red sports car driving around a track. It's flying down the stretches, speeding round the curves, smooth, low to the road, the engine racing...BUT...it has no brakes. It can't stop when the driver wants it to stop. It can't slow down to a safer speed. It may get off the track, or even crash! It will certainly have a hard time proving to everyone what it really can do.

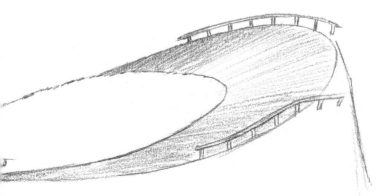

If you have *attention deficit hyperactivity disorder* (ADHD), you may be just like that racing car. You have a good engine (with lots of thinking power) and a good strong body, but NO BRAKES.

What Is ADHD Like?

Kids with attention deficit hyperactivity disorder may have any or all of these problems:

♦ Trouble focusing on just one thing

♦ Trouble paying attention

♦ Trouble thinking before acting

♦ Trouble keeping still

♦ Trouble keeping track of things

♦ Trouble learning in school

Trouble focusing on just one thing

Kids with ADHD often have trouble focusing on just one thing. Other thoughts, sights, or sounds keep interrupting. When you are taking a math test, other thoughts may interfere and keep you from concentrating on the test. It may be hard to listen to your teacher when there are so many other things to pay attention to in the classroom. You may be playing with the pencil on your desk, or watching the man mowing the lawn outside, instead of paying attention to the lesson. A bird singing outside the window may keep you from hearing the homework assignment.

Kids say it's like switching channels on a TV, and not being able to stay tuned in to one channel. You don't get to know very much about what is going on. When lots of thoughts keep popping into your mind, one right after the other, they can interfere with what you are trying to do.

Trouble paying attention

If you have trouble staying tuned in or paying attention to any one thing for more than a few minutes, you have a short attention span. This is where the first part of the name ADHD comes from: *attention deficit* hyperactivity disorder.

We all find it easier to concentrate when we are interested in something, so paying attention may *not* be a problem when you are doing something that you like. You may find it much easier to focus when the subject interests you, but feel quite lost when the topic is difficult or uninteresting. Your parents and teachers may be confused by this and think you should be able to pay attention all the time.

You may get angry when an adult keeps telling you to pay attention, especially when you feel that you are trying very hard to attend. The results may not be as good as you (or your parents or teachers) wish.

Trouble thinking before acting

Sometimes you may do or say things without thinking. You may ride your bicycle through your mother's garden, or call out the answer in class without raising your hand, or start a test before all the directions are explained. You may say the first thing that comes into your head, whatever it is!

Doing or saying something without thinking — with no brakes to stop you — is called impulsive behavior.

People usually ask, "Why did you do that?" You may not be able to explain, so you'll say, "I don't know." You may be able to discuss afterward what you did wrong, but you may forget to "think before you act" the next time. This can be very frustrating to the people around you, and to yourself.

Trouble keeping still

You may have trouble keeping still. You always have to be moving. Sitting in one place is very hard. You feel that you have to stand up, wiggle, or move around. Not being able to move may make you feel upset, tired, or sleepy.

If you are always moving and on the go, you may be hyperactive. This is where the second part of the name ADHD comes from: attention deficit *hyperactivity disorder.*

It is frustrating to be told over and over to stop moving, or to sit still. Like the race car that doesn't have any brakes, it is hard to stop even when you want to stop.

Trouble keeping track of things

Keeping track of belongings, school assignments, or your chores may be a problem. You may not know how to keep track of time or how to manage your time well. You may be disorganized in the morning and may suddenly discover you have run out of time. The bus has arrived, and you are not ready.

You may postpone school assignments until the last minute. You then have to rush. The work you turn in may not show all you really know. You might have done better if you had started earlier. You may then feel disappointed when you get your assignment back with many corrections on it.

Trouble learning in school

Because of all these problems, kids with ADHD may have trouble learning to read, spell, or do math. You may need to go to a tutor or to a special class for children with learning disabilities. You may need extra help, but you are just as smart as other kids.

Most kids with ADHD have lots of questions.

Why can I pay
attention better
on certain days?

How do I know
if I have ADHD?

Am I the only one
with this problem?

Is there something
wrong with my brain?

Why am I like this?

This book will try to answer your questions.

2.

HOW DO YOU KNOW IF YOU HAVE ADHD?

If you have some of the problems we have been talking about, you *may* have attention deficit hyperactivity disorder, but deciding who has ADHD is done only by professionals who are experts in this area. These may include pediatricians, psychologists, psychiatrists, and neurologists.

Everyone has some of these problems some of the time. It can be hard to pay attention in school when you are thinking about your birthday party that afternoon or about a new baby sister at home. These problems can become much worse if something very serious happens, such as your parents divorce or someone you love dies. The worry or depression you feel may cause you to be restless or irritable, for example.

But a diagnosis of ADHD would be considered only if your problems had existed for a long time and are not new ones, related to a stressful situation.

During an evaluation for ADHD, you may be examined by a doctor and tested on how you learn and on your ability to concentrate. The professionals will also talk to your parents and teachers and may ask them to fill out questionnaires.

After gathering all this information, the experts decide whether you have ADHD and recommend what can be done to help.

3.

ARE YOU THE ONLY ONE WITH ADHD?

Can you guess who in this class has ADHD?

You can't tell because kids with ADHD look just like everybody else.

About one in every 20 children has a problem with attention or hyperactivity. Over one million children in the United States are thought to have ADHD. A class of 20 might have at least one child with some form of ADHD. Both boys and girls can have ADHD. Some kids have an attention deficit without hyperactivity. They may be shy and withdrawn instead of hyperactive.

Although you may feel a little different from the other kids in your class, you have lots of company when you consider how many other children your age have this problem!

4.

WHAT IS GOING ON IN THE BRAIN?

The brain has several areas, each with its own job. The outside layers of the brain are called the *cerebral cortex*. Learning and thinking take place in this part of the brain.

Under the cortex is another area called the *subcortex*. This area contains the relay system which helps send messages to the thinking, remembering brain. It keeps everything on track and moving to the right station. The subcortex takes all of the information coming in and decides where it should go and what you should pay attention to now.

The brain is made up of nerve cells called *neurons*. These cells do not touch each other. There is a tiny space between cells called a *synapse*.

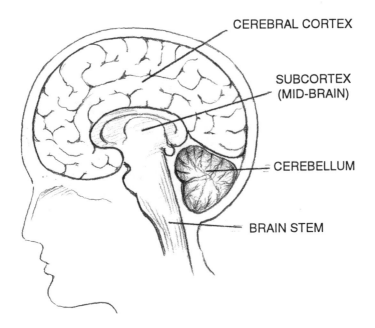

CEREBRAL CORTEX

SUBCORTEX
(MID-BRAIN)

CEREBELLUM

BRAIN STEM

The neurons relay messages across the synapse by chemical messengers. These messengers are called *neurotransmitters*.

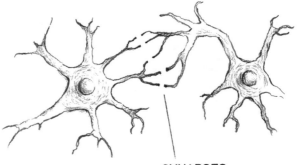

SYNAPSES

Have you ever felt like this?

Scientists have several explanations or theories for why this happens to you. One explanation comes from a recent study done at the National Institutes for Health in Bethesda, Maryland. This study found that there was less activity in the areas of the brain that control attention and concentration in people with ADHD.

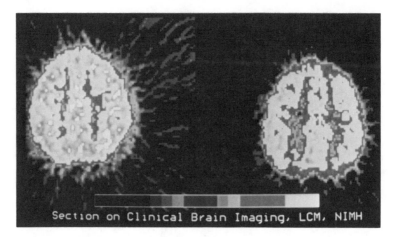

Section on Clinical Brain Imaging, LCM, NIMH

Figure reprinted by permission of *The New England Journal of Medicine, 323,* 20, 1991, and through the courtesy of Alan J. Zametkin, M.D.

Here are pictures of two brains from this study. The one on the left is the brain of an adult *without* ADHD. The one on the right is the brain of an adult *with* ADHD. The decreased brain activity shows up in these pictures as the darker areas.

Other scientists believe the chemical messenger system is not working properly. The brain may not have enough neurotransmitters to relay messages consistently. Scientists do not yet know why this happens, but it could be the reason for some of your attention and behavior problems.

It is important to understand that these theories are about chemical activity in the brain cells. These problems with brain activity levels and the neurotransmitters *do not affect intelligence.* Kids with ADHD are just as smart and healthy as other children.

5.◆

WHAT ARE
YOU FEELING?

Kids with ADHD have lots of different thoughts and feelings. Sometimes they feel:

Confused	Impatient
Overloaded	Scared
Angry	Dumb
Frustrated	Teased
Misunderstood	Anxious
Picked on	Lost
Forgetful	Tense
Unpopular	Hyper

What feelings do you have?

Let's look at some of these feelings.

You may feel *confused* or *lost* if you tune out and miss important pieces of information. Even if you look and listen carefully, some of the information just never gets into your brain.

You may feel *overloaded* if too much information comes in at one time.

You may feel *impatient* if you are impulsive. It's hard to wait. You start things before you fully understand what to do. You may feel *hyper* when you have to sit still. You may rush through assignments at school without checking them afterward. This may result in many careless errors and low grades. You may feel *frustrated* and *angry* because you really knew the right answer.

You may find it hard to study and take tests. Even when you review the material ahead of time, the information somehow "disappears" by the time the test begins. Then you may feel *forgetful* and *dumb.*

If this happens often, you may feel *scared* or *anxious* when you know you have a test coming up. When you feel *tense,* it is even harder to pay attention.

You may feel *picked on* if your parents scold or nag you more than your brothers or sisters. Your impulsive behaviors may sometimes be unsafe. You may need more reminders than other family members. Your parents care about your safety and happiness. They try to help you do the things they think are best for you.

You may feel *unpopular.* If you often say or do things before you think, other kids might not want to be with you. If you cannot wait your turn or follow the rules when you are playing games, other kids may not want to be your friend. If you are messy or can never sit still, you may be *teased.* All this can make you feel *misunderstood.*

Now for the good news! Kids with ADHD also feel:

Energetic	Curious
Athletic	Special
Creative	Artistic
Sensitive	Humorous
Attractive	Imaginative
Smart	Enthusiastic
Friendly	Adaptable
Caring	Happy

What are your feelings?

Along with all the problems of ADHD, there are also some surprising gifts. You can use your extra *energy* and *enthusiasm* in many positive ways. You may love to run and jump, play sports, or dance. You may be a good *athlete*.

You may be a very *creative* person and have many good ideas. Your *curiosity* and *imagination* may help you think and do things in ways that other people may truly envy. You may be an *artist*.

You may have a good sense of *humor* and make other people laugh. You may be especially *sensitive* and *caring* and very aware of other people's feelings. You may like to help people and be a good *friend*.

And, of course, ADHD kids are as *attractive, smart, special,* and even as *happy,* as anyone else.

Because you have had to deal with the problems of ADHD from an early age, you have a head start on other kids. You have the advantage of knowing your strengths and weaknesses. You are used to working hard to accomplish a goal. This ability to *adapt* and cope may be a real gift for you.

Now that you have learned more about ADHD, the next part of the book will tell you some ways you can put on the brakes and feel more in control of your life.

PART II
◆
GAINING
CONTROL

6.

GETTING SUPPORT

We all need people in our lives who are able to see what is special about us and to give help when things feel hard. Kids with ADHD need support as well. It is important to know that you don't need to manage everything alone. There are many ways to find extra help. Here are some of the ways ADHD kids have found support:

"My family helps me out by listening to my problems and working on homework with me."

◆◆◆

"I call my grandmother in another city once a week. She is happy to hear about all the good things I've done and gives helpful advice when I have a problem."

"I meet with my teacher or counselor at school several times a month to talk over problems. I also use the time to let them know how school has been going and how I've been feeling."

◆◆◆

"My doctor helps me. She prescribes medication to help me concentrate and pay attention."

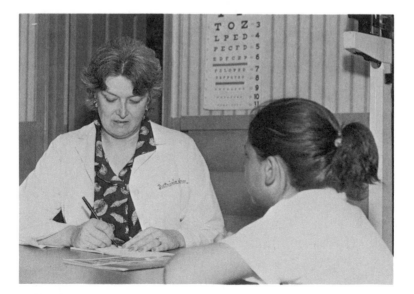

"I meet in a group of kids with a therapist who helps us understand our problems and feel good about ourselves. He also works with our families to learn new ways to help us."

7.

MAKING FRIENDS

Now that you have learned more about ADHD and about getting support, you probably understand yourself better. Now it is time to work on making and keeping friends. This will make you feel even better.

Let's think about what makes someone a good friend.

A friend

shares some of your interests
shares toys, ideas, or activities
is kind and thoughtful
listens to what you say

Find someone in your class or neighborhood who you feel comfortable with and who is interested in some of the same things you are. When you are first getting to know each other, plan to be together for only a little while, until you learn more about each other. Work together to make up the rules of your games beforehand, and don't change them once a game begins. Remember that not everything should always be done your way. Be flexible and try your friend's ideas some of the time.

Since acting impulsively may be a problem for you, try hard to slow down and think before acting. Look at the situation and try to think of two ways you could respond. Choose the "friendlier" one.

Good friends are kind and considerate. Make

it a habit to say something nice about the other person each time you are together. When you are thoughtful of other people, you will be surprised by how often they are nice to you in return.

Some kids do better with planned activities such as bowling, baseball, scouting, 4H, or other youth activities. An adult supervising can help keep things running smoothly at home with a friend or during a group activity.

If something goes wrong, discuss it afterward with your parents or counselor. With their help, try to come up with other ideas and solutions. You could practice with them some ways to act differently next time.

8.

UNDERSTANDING MEDICATION

For some ADHD kids, the doctor may prescribe medication. The medicine improves the way the brain works. It can help you concentrate and pay better attention, which can improve your behavior and learning.

Here is what some ADHD kids have said about their medication:

— "It helps me think one thought at a time."

— "It's like glue—before my thoughts were in pieces. The medicine stuck them all together."

— "I feel more organized."

— "It helps me calm down."

— "It helps me not climb the walls or 'spaz out' or get in trouble."

— "It helps me pay attention better."

— "My brain was cloudy, and now it's cleared up."

— "It lets me show how smart I am."

— "It helps me get my work done."

— "After 30 minutes, the ADHD just packs up and moves out."

— "It is my 'memory' or 'concentration' pill."

— "It is my brain-aid, just like a band-aid for my brain."

If your doctor has prescribed medicine for your ADHD, it is important that you learn as much as you can about it. The medicine can help you be more organized and focused. It can help you remember the rules at home and at school. It can help you have more control over what you say and do. It can help you pay better attention during class and after-school activities.

Usually kids need to pay attention all day—both at school and at home. You may take a pill after breakfast in the morning. The medication starts working in 20 minutes and lasts about 4 hours. If the effect of the medicine has worn off by lunch, your doctor may recommend you take another pill at lunchtime at school. The school nurse may need to give this to you during the school day. If you need help concentrating on your homework after school, an additional pill may be prescribed by your doctor. A lot of ADHD kids find that this dose before homework helps them be more efficient and not take as long to finish the work.

Sometimes these medicines may make you not feel hungry, especially for lunch. It is important that you not lose weight. Eat a good breakfast and try to eat something at lunchtime. You can make up on lost calories by eating nutritious snacks in the afternoon and before you go to bed at night.

A few kids complain about a slight stomachache after they take the medicine. Be sure to tell your parents, doctor, or teacher if you have that problem. Eating some crackers or drinking a glass of water will usually make the feeling go away. You should also drink a whole glass of water or juice when you take the pill, instead of just a sip. That will sometimes help prevent the ache from coming in the first place.

Remember to tell your parents and doctor how you feel while you are taking the medicine so they can help you. Visit your doctor regularly while you are taking the medicine. She or he can check your height, weight, and blood pressure and do a blood test if needed to make sure you are healthy and growing well. People used to think that ADHD medication would cause a slowdown in growth, but

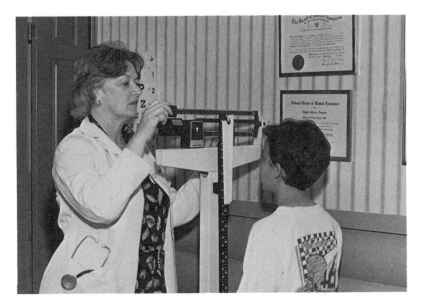

this has not been proven in studies that follow children for a long time.

All medicine needs to be prescribed and followed closely by your doctor. Your doctor is the person in charge of your medicine. You should take only as much as your doctor prescribes. However, you are an important part of the plan to help you do well. Make sure all your treatments are explained to you and that your opinions and questions are heard and answered. By following your progress closely, your doctor will be able to determine when and how much medicine you need. But you will know if the medicine is helping and when it wears off. Only you can tell your doctor how you feel.

BECOMING MORE
ORGANIZED

There are many things you can do to become more
in control of your life both at home and at school.
Here are some of the concerns ADHD kids often
have:

—How can I be better at following directions?
—How can I be a better listener?
—How can I become better organized and not
   lose things?
—How can I keep track of all the things
   I need to do?
—How can I manage my time?
—How can I stop being so messy?
—How should I study for tests?
—How can I make my work look better
   and neater?

These questions will be answered in the following
sections.

Following Directions

When you cannot remember everything that your teacher tells you to do, try writing a few **key words** while the teacher is speaking. For example, your teacher is telling you about tomorrow's assignment. She says, "The work must be written in cursive. It should be at least two paragraphs long. Be sure to use correct quotation marks." You can jot down a few reminder notes to look at when you get home. The notes might look like this:

1. cursive
2. 2 paragraphs
3. use quotes

Let's try another one. Your math teacher says, "Open to page 39 in your book. Do section B in class now and section C tonight for homework. Remember to use pencil and graph paper." Your notes might look like this:

Math homework

1. page 39
2. section C
3. pencil
4. graph paper

If it is difficult for you to write words, you can try making a few **quick pictures** to help you remember something. Your mother says, "After dinner, feed the dog. Then clean up your desk." Your sketches might look like this:

Let's try another one. Your physical education teacher says, "Bring in your sneakers and shorts for gym tomorrow." Your sketches might look like this:

You may need to remind adults, such as your teachers, that it is hard for you to remember a lot of information when you are only hearing it. Perhaps they can write the information down for you. Or a classmate who writes quickly could **make some notes for you.** Who do you know like that? Ask them to help.

Managing Your Time

If you have trouble keeping track of time, use clocks, timers, and calendars to help. Before you start a task, take a guess at how long you think it will take to complete. Then **time yourself** and compare this time with your first guess. With practice, you'll get better at figuring out how long things take. You can keep a record of your progress on a sheet of ruled paper.

Project	Amount of Time	
	Guess	*Actual*
1. Math homework	40 minutes	20 minutes
2. Proofread book report	10 minutes	30 minutes
3. Complete spelling sentences	45 minutes	40 minutes
4. Clean backpack	2 minutes	20 minutes

Another idea is to use a **timer** when you know you have only a certain amount of time to do something. This can help you to stay on task rather than get sidetracked.

When you have lots of different things to do, it usually helps to **make a list.** Here are some lists that often come in handy.

Things to Do Today

1. Get permission slip signed.
2. Study for spelling test.
3. Practice part for the play.
4. Two pages in language workbook.
5. Clean hamster cage.

Other Things for This Week	Date Due
1. Current events assignment	November 7
2. Science test	November 8
3. Note cards for social studies report due	November 9

Report/Project Due After This Week	Date Due
1. Social studies report	Dec. 1
2. Collage for art	Nov. 16
3. Return health survey	Nov. 14

Use a large **calendar**, blackboard, bulletin board, or poster in your bedroom. If you have a long-term project due (such as a research report), make sure to write the due date on your calendar.

Break the job down into **smaller parts**, and write them on calendar days. Some examples might be:

1. Read one chapter today.
2. Work 25 minutes on the science fair project today.

Write each of these parts on your calendar so you will know what to do each day.

Try to **spread out** what you have to do so that no day becomes overloaded. It may be helpful to have a parent, teacher, tutor, or counselor work with you to show you how to pace yourself and how to break jobs down into smaller parts.

Organizing Your Things

If you have a messy bedroom, school desk, or backpack, you should get an adult to help you develop a better system.

One idea some ADHD kids find useful is to put many **shelves** into their closet or on their wall. Each shelf can be marked with the name of a particular item.

Colors can also help you organize your things. For example, you might put all math work in a red folder and history in a green folder. Or at home, you might put underwear in a drawer with a yellow sticker and t-shirts in a drawer with a blue sticker.

You could pick a **specific day and time** each week for cleaning out your backpack or desk. You might need to get an adult to help you with this, too.

Try keeping a **box** near the door of your house. You can use it for your school books when you come home. You can take them out to do homework, but put them back when you are finished. You can also put in anything you need for school the next day (such as your gym clothes, or a permission slip for a class trip). Everything will be in one place when you are ready to leave in the morning. This will help you be more organized each day.

Improving Study Habits

There are many different ways to study. Some ADHD kids learn better when they **review** or **discuss** material with a friend, parent, or tutor.

Others may **underline** or **outline** the most important information to be studied.

Some students study alone using a **tape recorder,** reading the most important points from notes or the book. They listen to these recorded notes over and over.

Some ADHD kids find **moving** helpful. They walk around while they read, or pedal an exercise bicycle.

Some kids need **quiet** and no distractions. Others need frequent **breaks** for snacks or just to move around.

Try studying in **different places** or positions and using different techniques to see what works best for you.

Improving Schoolwork

Some kids find it useful to sit near the **front of the room** to decrease distractions. Some teachers may help by using a prearranged **signal** to remind you to get back on track.

Before you pick up your pencil to do your work, it is a good idea to **read all the directions at least two times.**

It is important to **check** over your class work and homework. You want your teachers to see how much you really know, so show them work without careless errors.

Improving Proofreading

Look for mistakes in spelling, punctuation, and capitalization. Are all your sentences complete and do they make sense?

Read your paper from the **bottom up.** This may help you spot your spelling and grammar errors better.

Make a **game** of it. See how many mistakes you can find in five minutes.

Ask another child or adult **to read your work out loud** to you to help you find errors.

Type your work on a computer or typewriter. It will look better and make it easier for you to spot mistakes.

Use the **spell-check** program on your computer to help spot your spelling errors. You can also buy a small portable spell-check, which you can use in school.

Improving Test Results

Study for each test over a period of many days. This makes it easier to review. You'll also feel less nervous.

As you begin the test, take a **deep breath** and remember that you are prepared.

Don't pick up your pencil to start the test until you have **read all the directions at least two times.**

Keep a few pieces of **clean paper** on your desk when you take a test. If you find it hard to remember information, use the blank paper to jot down everything that does come into your head about the subject. This often helps bring back the material you studied.

Always **check over** a test paper completely before you hand it in. Wait a few minutes and then check it again.

PART III

◆

CONCLUSION

To the ADHD Boy or Girl:

We hope you now know more about taking control of your life and about how to put on the brakes.

You have taken a big step by reading this book and learning what attention deficit hyperactivity disorder (ADHD) is all about. You can use this knowledge to make many positive changes in your life. Having ADHD will not stop you from doing most things you want to do.

Reread any section of this book when you need it. You will continue to get ideas.

Encourage the people in your life (such as parents, sisters, brothers, other relatives, teachers, and classmates) to read this book and to learn more about ADHD and you.

Ask for help when you need it. There are many people around willing to help you. With your cooperation everyone can work together.

With hard work and a strong will, you can succeed. It is important to remember that although the suggestions in this book may seem like extra work, they are worth trying. Many ADHD kids have found them useful.

It helps to have someone else work with you on trying out new ideas. Be creative. Experiment. See what works for you and use it! You really can change and improve.

Your attention deficit hyperactivity disorder is just one part of you. Try hard to manage it, and you will have plenty of energy left over to enjoy the many other parts of life as well.

Best wishes,

Patricia O. Quinn, M.D.

Judith M. Stern, M.A.

GLOSSARY

♦

Attention Deficit Hyperactivity Disorder—A condition in a person of average or above-average intelligence that includes symptoms such as short attention span, distractability, impulsivity, and / or hyperactivity.

Blood Pressure—The pressure of the blood against the inner walls of the blood vessels. It can be measured by a cuff placed around the upper arm.

Brain—The major organ of the nervous system. It controls all mental and physical activities.

Brain Stem—A part of the brain that controls automatic functions such as breathing, heart rate, and blood pressure.

Cerebellum—A part of the brain that controls the movements of the muscles.

Cerebral Cortex—The outermost layer of the brain. Its networks are essential to higher thinking activities. It makes up 40% of total brain weight.

Counselor—A professional who works with children or adults to help them understand feelings and solve their problems.

Diagnosis—Technical identification and description of a condition or problem.

Impulsive—Acting or speaking without thinking.

Irritable—Overly sensitive or in a bad mood.

Key Words—The most important words.

Learning Disabilities—Difficulties in learning to read, write, or do mathematics which cause problems in school achievement.

Medication—Substances used to treat illnesses or to improve functioning of the body or brain. Current medications used for ADHD include: Ritalin, Dexedrine, Imipramine, Cylert, and Clonidine.

Neurologist—A medical doctor who is a specialist in the way the nervous system works. The nervous system of the body is made up of the brain, spinal cord, and nerves.

Neuron—A single brain cell composed of a cell body, dendrites, and an axon. Each neuron is a complex coordinator of many stimuli. Within the cell body and dendrites, there are specialized receptors that take in stimuli from other neurons.

Neurotransmitters—Chemical substances produced by brain cells that act as messengers. They cross the space (synapse) between cells and conduct a nerve message or impulse along a pathway.

Nutritious Snacks—Food that is healthy and good for you.

Pediatrician—A medical doctor who is a specialist in the health of children and adolescents.

Prearranged—Planned ahead.

Prescribe—To write direction for the preparation and use of a medicine.

Professional—A person with training and a degree in a particular area.

Psychiatrist—A medical doctor who specializes in helping people who are having difficulties with their behavior. Sometimes called a therapist, this doctor can also prescribe medication.

Psychologist—A doctor who talks with people to help them understand their thoughts, feelings, and behavior. Some psychologists also do testing to learn more about people so they can help them.

Relay System—A way of passing messages from one cell to another using electrical impulses.

Social Worker—A professional who works with children and their families to help them solve their problems.

Spell-Check—A program for a computer or small, hand-held machine that is used to find and correct spelling mistakes.

Subcortex—The area below and surrounded by the cerebral cortex. It coordinates incoming stimuli from the brain stem and other areas and sends stimuli to the cerebral cortex and other areas of the brain.

Synapse—The site of contact of one neuron with another. A microscopic space (extremely small; can be seen only with a microscope) between the neurons.

Therapist—A professional who works with children and adults to solve problems, understand feelings, or change behavior. A therapist can be a counselor, social worker, psychologist, or psychiatrist.

Theories—Explanations that have not yet been proved to be true.

Tutor—A person who works with children outside of class to help them learn to do better in school.

RESOURCES

◆

*THE "PUTTING ON THE BRAKES" ACTIVITY BOOK
FOR YOUNG PEOPLE WITH ADHD,*
by Patricia O. Quinn, M.D. and Judith M. Stern, M.A.
This widely acclaimed companion volume allows children
ages 8 to 13 to put their understanding of ADHD into action.
Pictures, puzzles, mazes, and more, spark and hold the
interest of young readers while teaching them skills that make
everyday living more manageable.

*ADD AND THE COLLEGE STUDENT: A Guide for High
School and College Students with Attention Deficit Disorder,*
edited by Patricia O. Quinn, M.D.
Contributions by physicians, psychologists, educators and
fellow students offer practical information and advice to help
young adults who have ADD effectively navigate the transition
to college life.

BRAKES: The Interactive Newsletter for Kids with ADHD,
edited by Judith M. Stern, M.A. and Patricia O. Quinn, M.D.
For children ages 8 to 15, this newsletter includes games,
puzzles, ideas, letters, and other resources and activities
designed to help children learn coping techniques. It also includes information and suggestions for parents and educators.

For information about any of the above, write Magination
Press, 750 First Street, NE, Washington, DC 20002, or
phone 1-800-374-2721.